11 Secret Habits of Successful People:

Copy These 11 Quirky yet Effective Daily Habits of Millionaires, Superstar Athletes, and High Profile Politicians to Grow Your Business, Get a Promotion or Simply Feel More Fulfilled In Life

Justin A. Parker

Table of Contents

Bluesource And Friends

This book is brought to you by Bluesource And Friends, a happy book publishing company.

Our motto is **"Happiness Within Pages"**

We promise to deliver amazing value to readers with our books.

We also appreciate honest book reviews from our readers.

Connect with us on our Facebook page www.facebook.com/bluesourceandfriends and stay tuned to our latest book promotions and free giveaways.

Don't forget to claim your FREE books!

Brain Teasers:

https://tinyurl.com/karenbrainteasers

Harry Potter Trivia:

https://tinyurl.com/wizardworldtrivia

Sherlock Puzzle Book (Volume 2)

https://tinyurl.com/Sherlockpuzzlebook2

Also check out our other books
"67 Lateral Thinking Puzzles"

https://tinyurl.com/thinkingandriddles

"Rookstorm Online Saga"

https://tinyurl.com/rookstorm

"Korman's Prayer"

https://tinyurl.com/kormanprayer

"The Convergence"

https://tinyurl.com/bloodcavefiction

"The Hardest Sudokos In Existence

(Ranked As The Hardest Sudoku Collection

Available In The Western World)"

https://tinyurl.com/MasakiSudoku

Introduction

Congratulations on beginning your journey to a better, more successful, and productive life!

Are you looking to take control of the direction of your life and improve your productivity, efficiency, and experience better outcomes? If you want to up your game, you've come to the right place.

We live so much of our lives in the realm of habit, reacting robotically to situations using hardwired programs that were built into our psyche decades ago by those around us. They might have been well-meaning, but our parents, teachers, and others were all programmed in the same way!

It's amazing how much of what we do is governed by the subconscious – by habit. Most of us aren't even aware of all the small things we do automatically that are holding us back and preventing us from reaching our full potential. The problem is that most of us have the wrong habits.

While most people go through life robotically, without the habits and behaviors that are necessary to take them to the top, there are those we all admire who are operating in the upper spheres of life.

Sure, some people get to the top by sheer luck or by inheriting wealth. But most get there through sheer will, competence, and determination. Unfortunately, blaming external circumstances for our lot in life seems to be something that's becoming more common. You can't control external circumstances, but you can control how you react to them.

In other words, they apply habits guaranteed to produce success day in and day out.

All the rest of us need to do is learn what these habits are and then apply them. At first, it's going to take some amount of work. When you're reprogramming your behaviors that take place at the level of the subconscious, changing the habits you've had since they were solidified in childhood will not be an easy task. But the more you apply the habits of successful people to your own life, the easier it becomes. Eventually, they will replace the habits you're now using that are holding you back.

We will begin the book by looking at why habits matter, and then check out some methods you can use to change your habits. We'll explore the Pareto principle – a little-known rule that governs all human behavior – and then explore the Ivy Lee method for improving productivity. Then we'll look at the role that daily gratitude plays in your life and outlook, and talk about the importance of planning and goal setting. And much more!

Chapter 1: Why Habits Matter

You may not be conscious of it, but underlying every action you take and every result you get, are *habits*. These are the actions that we take every single day that are guided by our subconscious. Some habits are small, but they can add up to big consequences. Let me illustrate with an example:

When I was in college, I had a habit of showing up late to class. As you might imagine, there are consequences to that kind of behavior, and my habit of showing up late was particularly acute if it was a morning class. Often, I would arrive on campus so late I'd just blow off the class entirely. One day, I paid the price for this, having missed a class; I also missed an announcement from the professor that an exam had been moved up, to take place one class period earlier. That day, I moseyed into the building, late as usual. By the time I got up to the third floor and walked into class, I was 20 minutes late. Everyone was in there busily trying to do their exams. Feeling embarrassed, I just turned around and walked out. You can guess what happened next. I got an "F" for that class and had to start over the following semester.

That is a small example of obviously careless behavior, but habits like that - big and small - add up in all of our lives to produce the results that we see. My example was obvious, but maybe some others failed a college course as a result of habits that aren't so obvious — small things you do each and every single day can add up to bad results.

Needless to say, in order to get through college, I had to reprogram myself. This took a lot of conscious effort to replace my long-time habit of being late for everything with a more productive way of doing things and showing up on time. Eventually, it paid off, and I actually managed to get an advanced degree

with a high GPA. But it's not like I am perfect now –
I continue to make mistakes, and even the best of the
best make mistakes. But the difference is, they use
them as learning experiences.

Where do habits come from?

Habits are automatic behaviors. They may need a
trigger to bring them out, or you may simply engage
in them day after day. In my case, my "late" habit
would time itself to whatever deadline I had. This
happened on a subconscious level, and it was also a
kind of an avoidance mechanism. I was chronically
late to a class that started at 9 AM, but I would have
been late by the same number of minutes had the
class been at 9:15 AM, 10 AM, or noon.

I never thought about showing up late or really knew
why I was late. It "just happened." That day, I was 20
minutes late to the exam (which I would have failed

in, anyway). I was even surprised. Of course, looking back now, I see what was really going on.

Of course, the real reason I would show up late to class or to a job was that I had a bad attitude. An attitude is at the core of all of our habits. The problem is, most of us aren't even consciously aware of the attitudes we are carrying around with us – attitudes that are negative or limiting, that express themselves through our bad habits.

Most People Are in Robot Mode

A robot operates blindly, according to instructions contained within its program. In fact, most people behave in the same fashion. Habits are nothing more than programmed, automatic responses. So how do we go about changing them?

First, we have to understand where habits come from, ultimately.

Have you noticed that you have a lot of different *attitudes* about things? Those attitudes dictate how you feel and ultimately control your behavior. Years ago, I had a bad attitude about sitting in class. It manifested in my life via the habit of showing up to class late or skipping class (I often came so late I used being late as an excuse just to skip class). In order to change my behavior, I had to change my attitude first. It's not always easy to make the connection, but if you have a habit you don't like, you might try spending some time examining the attitudes operating behind the scenes creating the given habit.

So where do these attitudes, and the behaviors they generate, come from in the first place? A robot has to be programmed by an engineer. When we are small children, we're being programmed, too. First, it's by our parents, and indirectly, we are being programmed by the attitudes that exist in the society at large and in any subculture we live in. Our siblings also contribute to our programming. When we start going to school, we get programmed by our teachers and our peers. You can develop attitudes of success, failure, contempt, or compassion through these experiences. They get pushed down into the subconscious, and as you get older, many attitudes are completely baked in, and they generate many of our behaviors. We call these behaviors "habits." I like to think of our core attitudes and beliefs as programs so that they are analogous to the programs the engineer puts into a robot to make it function in a certain way.

Behaviors as Habits

So the things we do each day, whether it's an action we take, something we say, or a path we choose, are controlled by subconscious programs that were created over the years. Most of our behaviors are "programmed" during childhood, but you are still forming new programs as a result of your ongoing experiences.

You are going to find consistency across the attitudes you have, how they make you feel, and the actions that you take or behaviors you exhibit as a result of these programs.

Think about certain attitudes that have been baked into people that can determine whether or not they are going to start a business.

Do you believe you have control over your own fate and outcomes?

Or do you say "the rich get richer" or think the game is "rigged" for the one percent of society? Maybe you think the only way someone gets rich is through inheriting their money, winning the lottery, or from theft (or some combination thereof).

If you have the latter attitudes, then chances are that you're not going to be someone who starts a business. As a result, you might have different outcomes than your friend Mary, who believes that she is in control of her life and has an optimistic attitude. If we fast forward five years, you are probably languishing in the same job, still trapped by the same bitter attitudes, while Mary has doubled her income.

We don't always behave as dictated

In the beginning, I hated going to class, but I knew that from a practical standpoint, if I didn't force myself to go, I would completely flunk out of college and end up not getting a degree. So, I forced myself to start showing up to class on time. In the beginning, I still had the same grouchy attitude in class, but I was there anyway, and I was forcing myself to do my homework and other tasks required to pass the courses.

So, my attitude underneath was the same, and I would even feel physically ill or fatigued at first when I would enter the classroom. But I kept going.

The point of this little story is that we can literally change our behavior despite our underlying attitudes and feelings. You are not a prisoner of your habits. You direct them instead. At first, it's difficult to pull this off, but if you direct your conscious attention to a habit that you don't like, you can change it. You have the ability to change your behaviors, no matter how it makes you feel.

You've probably done this a million times already, in situations large or small. When your parents sent you to swimming lessons, many of you hated jumping off the diving board into the deep end of the pool – at least at first. But you forced yourself to do it anyway.

The conscious mind can choose how you act in the real world, despite your underlying attitudes and emotions.

Often, something amazing happens. Your feelings about the given action begin to change. Maybe you're not so nervous about jumping off the diving board any more, and rather than feeling anxious about it, you start feeling the anticipation.

Going back to my problems with attending class in college, after a few months of forcing myself to attend class, I began to enjoy it. I began to embrace learning and became excited about it.

So, what happened? First, I identified the behavior that was the apparent problem. This was my showing up late or skipping class (the real problem was my underlying attitude about it). I used my conscious mind and willpower to change my behavior, even though my emotions/feelings and attitude didn't want to come along. But with time, the application of my conscious control changed my underlying attitude.

Choose the way you behave and think

Maybe you have a problem of being late, or you are disorganized. But you accept it – it's "just the way I am." You can begin to change your bad habits by changing the way you think. Then change your behavior – even if it makes you uncomfortable.

In the beginning, you can't control your underlying feelings and attitudes. Those take place at a subconscious level. So, this is about training your subconscious. Remember, the subconscious operates on all those programs that have been "installed" throughout the years. Our task to change bad habits is to use our conscious mind and change the behavior controlled by those programs. You can think of it as "reprogramming."

Start with 3 Simple Bad habits

I want you to identify 3 bad habits in your life. Try and make them habits that aren't too complicated. We want to start simple while we are learning. Write them down, and for each habit, write down one or more underlying attitudes that you have that may be leading to the behaviors. This might not be as easy as you think, but hopefully, you can at least come up with one attitude.

Then over the next seven days, put conscious effort into behaving in a different way. If you don't like these habits – which I am assuming you won't – then change the behaviors. See if your underlying attitudes start shifting if you have changed the bad habit behavior over the course of a week or so.

Awareness and Responsibility

You alone are responsible for your own bad habits. They may have been programmed into you years ago. Maybe you had a bad teacher that convinced you that you were stupid, or "less than." That teacher is long gone. In the here and now, you and only you are responsible for the bad habits you are carrying out daily that may be keeping you from being successful, or as successful as you could be. If you don't like a bad habit, then change it.

Step one is awareness. Be aware of why you aren't successful in getting the job you want or having problems in relationships. Note the behaviors that are holding you back, and then change them.

The science of forming new habits

Honestly, I shouldn't have used the word "science." That makes it seem too complicated. But we know that habits, which are pre-programmed behaviors, operate under the realm of the subconscious. You have to use the conscious mind to change them with practice.

This is nothing unusual in human endeavors. Consider an expert pianist: Did they get that way by magic? Some people think so because they have incorrect thinking. Nobody gets anywhere by magic. Yes, it's true that some people are more talented than others, and some have more talents directed in a certain direction. However, you would be surprised at how much you can accomplish by simply practicing – practice, practice, practice. An expert pianist has practiced thousands, if not tens of thousands of hours, making it appear like magic. All that practice moved the act of playing the piano from the conscious mind into the realm of the subconscious, where body memory resides.

These thoughts were discussed in a book called *Outliers*. I didn't agree with every last detail of the book, and I think some people are gifted. But even gifted people put a tremendous amount of work into mastering their skills. Those that don't will never reach the top even if they have innate talents.

In the beginning, playing the piano can be a strenuous activity. You have to devote enormous amounts of energy into concentration, directing each finger to go to the right place at the right time. You may feel physical tension that comes about from the application of the will to direct your body in a way it's not naturally inclined to go.

But the more repetition you put into learning a new craft, the easier it becomes to carry it out. Soon, a budding piano player can play the instrument while hardly thinking about it. The more they practice, the less they have to think about playing, and the more they simply experience it as their subconscious mind takes over the work. When the subconscious mind takes over something, your conscious mind can take a break. Activities that you've put a lot of practice into are easier to carry out. Because of the will of the conscious mind – which imposed itself through the long hours of practice – the behavior has become a habit.

If you don't know how to play the piano now, you could learn. In the same way, you can learn new habits. In the beginning, carrying out the new habits is going to require a great deal of mental effort through the conscious part of the mind. But repetition will turn the new behaviors into habits.

Be Aware of Acquiring New Bad Habits

Even though you may be grown and think you are relatively fixed in your behaviors, you can not only still learn new good habits, you can also acquire bad habits even now. A part of becoming more productive, successful, and efficient is recognizing that you can pick up these bad habits. Having some awareness of this can help you avoid developing even more problems that you have to deal with.

Summary: Changing bad habits

So let's take a step back and summarize the process to follow in order to change bad habits. It's really only three steps:

- Awareness: Become aware of your bad habits and the attitudes underlying the habit that causes you to exhibit negative behavior.

- Conscious will and practice: Make a conscious effort to exhibit the behavior that you want to become a new habit. The more attention and practice you put into it, the faster the behavior will enter into the realm of the subconscious and become automatic. Remember, just like a new piano player, repetition is how we learn anything new.

- Affirmations: Use visualization and affirmations to help shape your behaviors. This is a way to communicate with your subconscious. You need to use repetition here as well.

Chapter 2: How to Effectively Change a Habit

Visualization and affirmations are important for sure, but if you want to change habits effectively so that the change actually takes place and sticks, you need to take practical steps in the real world. That means consciously changing your behaviors. In this chapter, we are going to develop a 10-step plan that can be used to help you effectively change any bad habit.

Know what your bad habits are and where you are going

The first step is to actually know what your bad habits are. Start by keeping a "habit journal" and write down a list of all the habits that you want to change. But don't stop there – you should also write down the habits that you want to replace them with. Using my simple example from the last chapter, the habit I would write down to change would be:

Showing up late

So the habit I would replace that with would be:

Showing up early

Identify emotions that underlie bad habits

Many emotions can be behind bad habits that are a part of our lives. For each bad habit that you identify, write down the emotional states or needs that may be driving the bad habit. Sometimes, bad habits are masking an underlying emotional need.

Some of the most important emotional states that are behind negative habits include:

- Feelings of inadequacy
- Fear of failure
- Guilt

- Anxiety

- Boredom

- Frustration

- Isolation or loneliness

- Stress

- Remorse

- Regret

- Anger

- Alienation

- Annoyance/Irritability

- Self-doubt

- Shame

- Insecurity

- Envy

- Jealousy

These emotional states can be rooted in attitudes that lead to bad habits, or they can be emotional states that trigger bad habits. For example, someone who is feeling lonely might be triggered to consume a large amount of alcohol by themselves, or they may waste a lot of time on the computer browsing "social" sites instead of going out to meet actual people.

In some cases, eliminating a bad habit might require a direct confrontation with a negative emotional state that you're experiencing.

Determine Behaviors that spring from negative emotional states

Next, we need to look at negative behaviors that arise from the negative attitudes and emotional states that lead to our bad habits. For example, someone who feels alienated may manifest this by leading a life with little direction or goal-setting. Someone whose life is ruled by insecurity may be a braggart.

Are you often worried or nervous or suffering from anxiety? Think about what underlying emotional states on the list in the previous section might be causing this.

An interesting bad habit is not getting enough sleep. Of course, there are genuine cases of insomnia, but some people are experiencing insomnia for other reasons. It could be caused by frustration that you're experiencing at work or in your relationships. Or maybe you're feeling frustrated because you're not making enough money to pay your bills. So, it's not as simple as just identifying a bad habit and saying you're going to replace it with a good habit; you might also need to really evaluate what is causing the negative emotional states in the first place. Getting rid of the bad habit might require fixing that first, so if you can't pay your bills such that you end up not getting enough sleep, a second job might be required for a while before you solve the immediate problem.

Dealing with the emotional state that leads to the bad habit

One of the first steps that will require a lot of conscious effort is identifying emotional states that lead to bad habits when they first occur. Is one of your bad habits eating late at night? What emotional state triggers the urge to do so? Learn how to identify it and then nip the bad habit in the bud.

Battle Negative Self-Talk with Positive Thoughts

All of us are swarming in negative self-talk, and we don't realize how destructive it can be. The first step is to become aware of the negative self-talk that may be filling your head, leading to bad habits. This is going to take a lot of conscious effort because this happens automatically. It's part of the programming that you've experienced your entire life. When you recognize negative self-talk taking place inside your head, you need to replace it with positive affirmations.

This idea is going to sound crazy at first, but I am going to throw it out there as something to try if you have a problem with negative self-talk. Wear a rubber band around your wrist. When you have a negative thought, snap the rubber band against your wrist, and then use a positive affirmation to counter the negative thought.

You will be surprised at how effective this method is in eliminating negative self-talk. If the rubber band idea sounds too much, try it without the rubber band. However, you might be missing out. It's surprisingly effective at sending a jolt to your subconscious mind (which is the driver behind the entire negative self-talk) to stop it. So the process here is awareness (identify when negative self-talk occurs), shock (generate minor pain), and replacement (swap out a negative thought for a positive thought).

Eliminate bad habits in stages

If you owe $50,000 in back taxes but have a middle-class income, would it be better to break it down into small payments and pay it off over time, or hope to come up with a get-rich-quick scheme so you could cut one check to the IRS?

Most of us would probably agree the best way to solve a big problem is to break it down into a set of small problems and solve each small problem. In the case of a bad habit, look and see if the bad habit is one that can be decomposed into multiple bad habits that, by themselves, are easier to eliminate.

Don't beat yourself up for setbacks

Setbacks are inevitable. You're not necessarily going to eliminate a bad habit the instant that you identify it. What's important is how you react to the inevitable mistakes. If you punish yourself with negative self-talk, you are only going to make it more difficult to overcome a lifetime of bad programming.

Identify triggers and eliminate them if possible

Bad habits often materialize when certain triggers appear in your life. Many times, the triggers will activate the negative emotions (jealousy, stress, insecurity, etc.) that lie behind your bad habits. Ultimately, you want to be able to replace a bad habit by a good habit and have this happen even when the triggers are present. However, during the transformation phase, sometimes, it can be helpful to eliminate the triggers.

Seek out successful people

Sometimes, it helps to be around people who are better than you are and let their vibe rub off on you. Someone once told me that you are who your friends are, so it makes sense to hang around the successful if you can. They can help you develop good habits, internalize them and also serve as examples.

Use Visualization, but don't count on it

Visualization can be a very productive tool, but it can't change things by itself. I am not a believer in magical thinking, and believe that practical steps that you take ACTION on are ultimately what will change your bad habits. That said, visualization is a tool you can use to reinforce your efforts and help you replace bad habits with good habits. Each time you catch yourself about to engage in a bad habit, or actually carry it out, take some time to visualize yourself engaging in the opposite – a good habit.

Chapter 3: Focusing on What Really Matters

There are bad habits, and then there are BAD HABITS that are really holding you back from being as successful as you can be. Sometimes, how bad a habit depends on the circumstances in which the bad habit is carried out. I've been using being late as an example of a bad habit. Suppose that you are working for a big Wall Street firm in New York City. If you routinely show up 20 minutes late for meetings, you're going to get into major trouble and might even lose your job. On the other hand, if you are self-employed with a passive-income based business, if you sleep late several days a week, it probably has no impact at all.

So the magnitude of the bad habit really depends.

Also, if we list all of our bad habits, we are going to find that some are more impactful than others. When you list all of your bad habits, try arranging them by the impact it gives you. Assign a score from 0-100 for each bad habit and its impact on your life. Don't use external definitions on what is impactful or not. Use criteria for evaluation that depends on how the habits are affecting your life and yours alone.

Now think about what your goals are in eliminating bad habits: Is it earning more money? Being more productive? Getting a promotion? Completely changing the direction of your life?

Some people are completely overwhelmed by bad habits. I had a friend who had a habit of showing up late to class as I did in college. But he had a lot of other bad habits too, like being totally disorganized and ignoring his bills. It wasn't that he was a bad person or anything like that, but he would simply not pay attention to his bills, and they would start piling up. I am not sure where this comes from. Maybe his parents were over-attentive in taking care of his needs, and so he just didn't have the mentality of, "hey, you need to keep track of your bills and pay them regularly (a basic life skill)". He eventually ended up in bankruptcy. Since his bad habits were overwhelming, they were pretty serious, involving the last possibility, and completely changing the direction of his life.

Ranking the importance of bad habits

So what bad habits were the most impactful? That would require a detailed analysis. Maybe the fact that he was ignoring his bills might be deemed fundamental. One reason I'd pick that one is that bad habit is one that would generate chaos in his life later. If you don't pay your water and electricity bills for three months, or your mortgage, then all of a sudden (it seems to you) you have a crisis on your hand, and the magnitude of the problem has been transformed from a small one into a big one. So, bad habits have to be ranked for what their ultimate impact will be.

You are going to want to eliminate the habits with the biggest impact first.

The Pareto Principle

One of my favorite lessons in life is the Pareto Principle. This principle is about how productivity relates to human activity, but it also relates to bad habits. In a nutshell, it says that 80% of the spoils – in ANY human endeavor – go to 20% of the participants. Are you big on income inequality? Consider giving up your obsession. Income inequality is a natural result of human activity. A small (at least, relatively speaking) subset of individuals is always responsible for the vast majority of the productivity that occurs in any activity.

If you have 100 farmers, you will find that 20 of them produce 80% of the food.

If you have 100 real estate agents, 20 of them are going to earn 80% of the commissions.

If you have 100 business owners, 20 of them are going to earn 80% of the profits.

Of course, the exact numbers are going to vary. It's obviously not exactly 80/20 all the time or ever. The point is the underlying principle, which is that a small percentage of any groups are responsible for a vast majority of the productive output.

This works in other ways as well. If you are running a business, you will find that 20% of your customers are responsible for 80% of your revenue.

This is also true with bad habits. It turns out that a relatively small fraction of your bad habits is responsible for a large fraction of your negative outcomes. For the sake of argument, we will say that 20% of your bad habits are responsible for 80% of your bad outcomes. The exact numbers are not all that important; the point still stands.

So, let's take a step back and examine what that means. You probably already know the answer. No matter what your ultimate goal is – more productivity, moving up the corporate ladder, completely changing the direction of your life, earning more money – the fact is, you can get 80% of the way toward your goal by eliminating just 20% of your bad habits.

The challenge, of course, is to look at your life and determine what those 20% of bad habits are. But the importance of making this identification is crucially important. The more successful and accurate you are in figuring out what bad habits are the most impactful, the faster you can reach your goals, no matter how lofty those goals are.

Think back to my friend with the problem of ignoring his bills. After a few months of doing this, all of a sudden, he needed a few thousand dollars at once. He is contacting everyone he knows, wondering if he could borrow some cash from them so he could catch up on his bills. Of course, he can't get a loan because of his history of late payments, so it's the side effect of his one bad habit that has magnified his fundamental problem. If he just changed this one bad habit and paid his bills once a month, it would reverberate throughout his entire life, and he would be more successful overall.

Determine where to spend time and effort

We all have to face one reality in the universe – time is, by far, the most precious commodity. So, if you are trying to improve your success, productivity or whatever it is, you want to use that time wisely. That is why it's important to become aware of the Pareto principle. It doesn't matter what you are doing, what area you work in, where you live, or even what your system of government is – a small number of the activities you engage in are going to produce BIG results. So in the case of the topic of this book, a small percentage of your bad habits are having a big impact on your life, so you want to allocate your time fixing your bad habits to those 20% of things that matter the most.

Remember: If you can break down a big bad habit into a set of small bad habits

In some cases, your bad habit can be broken down into a set or series of smaller habits that add up to the one bad habit. To choose an obvious example, my friend who had a problem paying bills wasn't paying his house payment on time, wasn't paying his car payment on time, wasn't paying his utilities on time, wasn't paying his credit cards on time, and so on. Let's also note that he had 4 personal loans he had taken out (as a result of his need to come up with cash periodically to catch up on his bills).

OK, so what? Well, we can rank all his bills by priority. For example, it's probably most important to have shelter, and then after that, you might put water and electricity. Further down the list would be credit cards.

We can view his bad habit of not paying bills as a sequence of bad habits. To rectify the bad habit and not only promote better habits but avoid immediate problems, we can apply the Pareto principle and identify the 20% of habits that are most important. Not paying a credit card for a few months isn't good, but it's not catastrophic in the same way that losing your home or having the water shut off is. Also, the home mortgage is a LARGE bill compared to the others.

So, if I could counsel my friend today, the first few months of coaching I would spend focusing on those bills that has the most impact on his very survival, and so would cause the most chaos by not paying them. In other words, he could eliminate 80% of his problems by focusing on paying 20% of his bills – say his home mortgage and utility bills to start.

Once he got caught up on those, then we could widen the circle to eliminate more bad sub-habits – those bills that are not as critical for survival or amounts to smaller amounts of money.

The Pareto Principle Applies ANYWHERE

I've been using an example of someone with a personal problem in order to illustrate the Pareto principle, but it can be applied anywhere in any endeavor. Are you in sales? Maybe you are paying too much attention to customers that aren't the most productive. You might be able to increase your commissions by focusing more on that 20% of customers that generate 80% of your commissions. Or maybe you have efficiency issues. Are 20% of your tasks taking up 80% of your time?

Instead of trying to save time generally, you might need to focus on looking at making a subset of your tasks more time efficient.

Or you can take a look at what works and emulate it. Suppose that you have a video game business. You would (inevitably) find that 20% of your games made 80% of the company's revenue. How would you use that information? One way, of course, would be to devote all of your sales energy to pushing the subset of games that generate the most revenue, while ignoring the others.

But an alternative strategy would be to find out what characteristics of those 20% of games made them so successful in the first instance, and then apply those to the other games. This could be described as moving the goal posts. Of course, then you create a new situation because it's always going to be the case that the Pareto principle always applies, so you will still end up with a small fraction of them making most of the money. But you will already be in a better situation because you will have raised the average.

Chapter 4: Ivy Lee Method

Each day, whether at work or even in your home life, you face multiple tasks that need to get done. They all vary by complexity, priority, and deadline date. In order to have the most productive day possible, you need to optimize your organization to get your tasks done in the most efficient manner.

There are many strategies that you could use: Some people prefer to bang out the easiest tasks first. That way, you ensure that you get multiple easy tasks out of the way so that at least something was completed in the event that the more complex, difficult, or time-consuming tasks run into a snag, leaving you in a situation where you don't get anything done.

You could use an analogy that you were assigned to read books of 20 pages, 50 pages, 125 pages, and 500 pages. If you jump in on the 500-page book first, you might not finish it and may end the day without completing a single book. But if you start with the smaller books first, you could complete the 20-page, 50-page, and 125-page books, and even if you didn't get far with the 500-page book on the first day, at least, you got the other ones out of the way.

Other people live by the strategy of tackling the most complex and difficult tasks first. Using this strategy, you make headway in your big task, leaving less overall work ahead.

Of course, there are many other factors involved in the real world, such as deadlines. Continuing with the book analogy, if your 125-page book is due within 24 hours and the 20 and 50-page books aren't due until five days later, obviously, you are going to prioritize the 125-page book.

In either case, ultimately, the goal is to get as much done as possible in the shortest amount of time. Many people look to improve efficiency to avoid spending unnecessarily long hours at the office. Everything you do in life comes with a cost, and one of the costs of a professional job is getting your tasks done in a proficient and productive manner and putting in the necessary time to get things completed. However, another price you have to pay is time away from family and personal matters. Nobody said that they want to die at the office, so if you can get more done in less time, it benefits everyone – including your employer.

Having a reasonable workload

Nobody is superhuman, and in order to have sustainable productivity, you need to have a reasonable number of tasks that you can get done. This is the core of the Ivy Lee method, which was developed in the early 20th century, but is as relevant now as it was then. This method can be summarized as attacking your productivity problems in three areas:

- Breaking work down into a fixed number of tasks.
- Prioritizing tasks to get the important stuff done first and improve efficiency.
- Planning ahead.

Step 1: Prepare the night before

If you were planning to invest for your retirement, you would probably agree that putting a small amount of money down early is better than waiting until a few years before retirement and scrambling to build up several hundred thousand dollars over a short time period. The same principle applies when trying to make your workday as efficient as possible, and that is the basis of the first step of the Ivy Lee method.

The Ivy Lee method is focused on having six tasks to perform at the office each day. In order to save time later, the night before, you determine what the six tasks are, and then rank them by priority. The most important task is what you'll tackle the first thing in the morning.

You can do your planning either in the evening before you leave the office, or at home later at night before going to bed. Either way is fine – the important thing to note about this is that you have planned out your next day at the office ahead of time.

The Ivy Lee Method is Linear

The Ivy Lee method seeks to avoid "multitasking," and instead, uses a linear approach to getting things done. So, when you get to the office the next morning, you start on task #1 and do not do any work on any of the other tasks until task #1 is completed.

When task #1 is wrapped up, then you move to task #2 and apply the same rule.

No overworking allowed

Balance is one of the keys to a successful life, and the Ivy Lee method has balance built-in. Unless there is a critical task, you can end your workday when it ends and simply push off any unfinished tasks to the next day. So, if you only got through tasks 1,2, and 3 on Monday, then tasks 4,5, and 6 are moved to Tuesday. Depending on what new tasks have come into the mix, they can be reordered by the new priority.

This way, you avoid paying the price of working yourself to death and not spending time with family and so forth outside the office. Being a workaholic might help you climb the ladder, but being more productive is better than destroying your life, putting in a lot of long hours. That isn't to say you shouldn't be working hard and putting in the extra when absolutely necessary, but you should aim for balance and making yourself more valuable to your employer or customers through increased productivity.

Eliminate Indecision

Many people don't plan at all – they just show up to work and start doing whatever comes to mind. This can lead to indecision paralysis for some. One advantage of the Ivy Lee method is that it gets rid of indecision problems. You've planned out your tasks ahead of time and have it set down in writing what you are going to do at work that day. By removing this indecision issue and planning things out ahead of time, you've already increased your productivity and avoided wasting large amounts of time during the workday.

Of course, this is idealistic

In the real world, situations often change on the ground. When you get to the office, your boss (or clients, if you are self-employed) may throw something new at you, and often, a manager (or the situation, if you are self-employed) will blow everything up by demanding that you work on something else. However, for a large fraction of your time, it's probably the case that you will be able to apply the method, so even if you can't rely on the Ivy Lee method all the time, it should work to add a lot of productivity and reduce the amount of time you have to spend working to get things done.

Chapter 5: Giving Daily Gratitude

Giving daily gratitude – thanks for our blessings and for those around us, should be a part of everyone's daily habits. You can be resentful and jealous, and full of envy, or you can be full of joy and gratitude for what you do have even if you're not as successful now as you'd like to be. Giving daily gratitude will help to increase your optimism and inspire positive emotions. Remember one thing – you create your own reality. If you are wallowing in negative emotions because things are not as good as they could be, those negative emotions are going to be the energy that drives your results, and you'll either stay in the same rut or even find things getting worse. So, why not take a different path? By being grateful for what you have, you can have your life governed by positive thoughts, which will help guarantee future success.

Keep a Journal to Give Thanks

Keeping a journal is always a good way to keep an accurate record of events and how we felt about them. This is true when giving daily gratitude, as well. Consider keeping a daily gratitude journal where you can record your thoughts and feelings about things, people, and events that you are grateful for each day. Being able to refer back to the journal during times of stress, worry, or depression can help replace those feelings with more positive thoughts. You can also increase your sense of well-being and satisfaction by reviewing the journal periodically to see what you have been thankful for and to reinforce positive thoughts.

One of the benefits of a daily gratitude journal is that it will help you look at things more optimistically since you'll be putting in an effort to find new things to be grateful for each day.

When you choose to record your thoughts is up to you. Some people prefer to wait until the end of the day, while others like to do it first thing in the morning. You can record your gratitude any way you like – an online or smartphone app built to function as a diary can work for this purpose.

Share your gratitude

If you feel up to it, you can give your gratitude more energy by sharing it with others. You can do this with your immediate family or with friends and co-workers. This should be done judiciously, as you want others to feel appreciative, but at the same time, you don't want to come across as having flaked out. With family, if you have children, it can be a helpful tool for teaching your children to be thankful rather than jealous, envious, and resentful by sharing your gratitude with them and helping them think of what they are grateful for each day.

Gratitude in Work

When it comes to getting work done, no matter how talented and special you may be, most projects that are significant depend on the work and input of multiple people – often hundreds or even thousands of individuals. For that reason, gratitude towards others can help increase productivity and enhance teamwork.

One of the first elements necessary for building gratitude in the work environment is having trust in others. These days, this can be difficult since cynicism has become more of a rule than an exception. Maybe it's because society has been gradually becoming more fragmented and isolated with time. Negative views of others are also reinforced because, with more fragmentation and isolation, it seems that there are also more opportunities for con-artists and scammers to take advantage of people. I've also seen people con themselves into high authority positions in corporations when, in reality, they don't actually have the skill set necessary to do the job properly.

However, I would like to propose that you adopt an attitude of trust no matter how jaded you are. We are not talking about blind trust – you must hold others accountable. However, you can have a starting position where you see the good in people and trust them until proven otherwise. Until you catch someone in a lie, assume they are truthful and honest.

Acknowledge the contributions of others

When you recognize that the efforts of other members of your team created any success you are now enjoying, it's very helpful to be upfront about acknowledging their achievements. In the workplace, there is nothing that can go further in building a team spirit and reciprocity. The goodwill that is generated by following this approach will also heighten productivity and appreciation for your own efforts as well. Never offer phony praise or acknowledgment –

it should always be straight from the heart. People can definitely tell when you're trying to pull the wool over their eyes, and this is pretty clear when it comes to acknowledging contributions.

Some of the benefits of daily gratitude

We all have a sense that if you carry around a negative attitude every day, this is going to lead to ulcers, sleepless nights, and other problems. Does taking the opposite approach – that is expressing gratitude, offer benefits you can enjoy instead? You bet it does. Here are some of the benefits you can enjoy by taking an attitude of and actually expressing daily gratitude:

- Improved happiness
- Make new friends and build more professional contacts
- Have others appreciate you more
- Sleep better
- Improve your sense of well being
- Appreciate what you have

- Give you more motivation for improvement and growth
- Improved mental health
- Feeling happy more of the time
- Avoid feelings of resentment and other negative emotions
- You'll become a better leader

So, try a dose of daily gratitude, and see how it improves your life, both at home and at work.

Chapter 6: Wake Up Early

We hardly give a thought to the huge amount of time that we waste in our lives. When I look back on my life, in my early years, I wasted huge amounts of time literally doing nothing. I accomplished hardly anything; you could say my life was going nowhere fast. The time of day you wake up in the morning is one area where we can have a hard look at this. What if you woke up 30 minutes or an hour earlier in the morning and devoted that time to productive activity instead of trying to catch a few more zzzz's?

Can your time be put to more productive use?

A little exercise with arithmetic can help put things into perspective: If you decided to wake up 30 minutes earlier every single day, over the course of a year, that would be 10,950 minutes. Since there are 60 minutes in an hour, over the course of a year, simply getting up 30 minutes earlier every single day would net you an additional 182.5 hours of time. That turns out to be a little more than 15 hours a month.

Now, what if you devoted that time to start a new online business, instead of trying to inch in more sleep that would have dubious benefits anyway? An additional 15 hours a month spent on a new business could pay significant dividends by the year's end. It doesn't sound like a lot of time, but it's time you could spend productively without having much impact on the rest of your life from a cost perspective right now. But six months down the road, that little business might be bringing in $1,000 or $2,000 a month in passive income. If I told you that getting up 30 minutes earlier each day could increase your income by $1,000 a month, would you do it?

Of course, the time could be put to other uses as well. We all hear the mantra that education is a lifelong experience, and we should never stop learning. How many of us actually put that advice into practice? If you got up 30 minutes a day earlier than you did now, you could use that 30 minutes a day toward educating yourself in needed areas. You could spend 30 minutes each morning reading self-help books. If you're working in the technology sector, you could read books on the latest programming languages and techniques. If you're in management, you could read business-oriented books. Or maybe, you want to spend the time, no matter what you're into now, educating yourself for a future career change.

Follow the leaders

One thing that many of the world's top achievers have in common is getting up early in the morning and using their time productively. According to *Business Insider* magazine, most top CEOs of the world's leading companies are early risers. Getting up early gives you an edge over the competition and helps jump-start your productivity.

Getting up early also has other benefits: It will let you get the tasks you need to get done earlier and have more time later for personal pursuits and family time. The way that you spend your time early in the morning is up to you, but the many different ways you can spend it can have a positive impact on your day. Many people choose to get their exercise out of the way first thing in the morning. This helps you feel better and more energized, and then later in the day, you won't have to be thinking about carving out time to exercise. Instead, you can focus on the things that need to get done. Exercising first thing in the morning can also help sharpen mental clarity, making you more productive throughout the day. Many famous people at the top reaches of life begin their days with an exercise routine, from Michelle Obama to Richard Branson, to Tim Cook.

Jumpstart your productivity

The early hours also provide some quiet time that you can use to jumpstart your productivity. If you have tasks that need to be done first thing each business day, why not get up earlier and do them while everyone else is languishing in bed? Since most people are still asleep in the early morning hours, you can work without interruption, leading to higher efficiency. Getting up early can also offer the opportunity of being the first person at the office. Wait a minute! Did that make you uncomfortable? Maybe it did, but you ought to reconsider your attitude about work, if that's the case. One principle I've adopted is to do every job, no matter how small, to the best of my ability and to be enthusiastic about my work. It's amazing how much a change in attitude can accomplish, and if you're early to work, you can assure yourself of more success going forward.

Get more out of life

When you start adding up the seconds, minutes, and hours spent engaging in various activities, it can be quite stunning seeing how much time we actually waste doing nothing, essentially. We've already seen that if you get up 30 minutes earlier each day and devote that time toward a new online business, you're already putting 15 hours into the business. And prior to this exercise, that was probably 15 hours that you swore you didn't have. Now, what if you got up 1 hour earlier instead? Now, you've got 30 hours a month to work on the business. Add even more time, and you're really putting the time in that could actually create a money-making exercise.

Reducing time spent sleeping isn't the only way that we waste our time. I recently read that Americans are spending up to 11 hours per day interacting with media of some kind. Up to five hours are spent watching television alone, and you need to add a lot more to that, including time spent reading silly posts on Facebook, arguing with people on Twitter, and playing video games. Think about what that means: Are an extra 30 minutes browsing on Facebook rather than spending actual face-to-face time with your family or partner worth it? You only have one life to live; how you spend your time is up to you, but here is a fact: Your time on Earth is rapidly running out.

So, imagine now that we cut into some of that TV-watching time. If we can find an hour to work on a new business or to learn a new skill in the morning, the fact that so much time is utterly wasted indicates that we can heighten our productivity even more, by taking some time in the evening to devote to productive activities. If you just took 60 minutes in the evening to work on your new business rather than wasting time seeing people's cat videos on YouTube or what people are saying on Facebook, now you'd have two hours per day spent on your new business – and more time invested means that success is more likely.

Time wasted adds up. Consider that the average lifespan is around 80 years, and suppose that we consider someone who is already 40 years old. That means they have 40 years left in their life, if they are lucky (if this is you, we hope that you live well beyond 80!) What if between now and then, you devote 3 hours a day to social media pursuits, whether its viewing photos on Instagram, reading Facebook posts, or arguing with people you'll never meet on Twitter? How much time is that exactly? Well, three hours a day is 1,095 hours a year. A full-time job is, on average, considered to be 2,080 hours a year, so you can see that your social media pursuits are like having a part-time job, but you're not getting any money out of it. Over 40 years, that would be 43,800 hours ogling over Facebook posts (of course, who knows if Facebook will last that long?) Truth be told, 43,800 hours is around five years of time.

Do you really want to spend five years out of your life looking at social media posts?

In the long term, if you spent that activity on productive pursuits rather than meaningless entertainment, you would free up time *later on*. Failing to invest in things now for deferred gratification is a huge problem that holds many people back from success.

Chapter 7: Avoid Short-Term Thinking

While many characteristics and habits separate the successful from the rest of us, the disease of short-term thinking is one that deserves an honorable mention. It may surprise you, but many people will opt for short-term benefits over long-term benefits every time. In fact, *most* people will do so. Life is full of trade-offs, and this is one of the most important trade-offs of all. Short-term thinking is a part of what we can call the "poverty mindset" that plagues millions of people.

It turns out that being able to take the long-term benefit over the short-term benefit is a marker of maturity. Studies of small children have shown that this is the case. It's really hard for small children to give up the enticement of a piece of candy now in exchange for the promise of a large ice cream sundae or much larger candy bar in the future. This trait also goes back to our evolutionary past. Studies of monkeys and other primates show much of the same thought process.

One famous test that was given to small children was the marshmallow test. A child would be left in a room with a single marshmallow on a table. They would be told that they could eat that one now, or wait for 15 minutes and then they'd be given two marshmallows. As you might guess, a lot of children found this task to be impossible to perform successfully. They would give in to their impulses and eat the marshmallow, giving up the better future where they would have twice as many marshmallows to enjoy.

Some children were able to wait the 15 minutes out and get the second marshmallow as a reward. The researchers followed these children into adulthood and found out some very interesting correlations. The children who exhibited characteristics of being able to engage in delayed gratification behavior by waiting out the 15 minutes to get the second marshmallow were the ones who ended up succeeding as they grew up. They were the ones that got better grades, better SAT scores, and went to college and to better universities.

While we might be dismissive and note well that's how kids think, the fact is that most people fail to really outgrow that type of thought process. And failing to think in terms of "delayed rewards" has trapped tens of millions of people into lives of poverty and mediocrity.

Consider a thought experiment: What if the government seized all the money currently in circulation and said we were all starting over from scratch? What would happen to all the rich and poor people? In five years, we'd probably come back and see that, by and large, the same people that were rich before all the money was seized were rich. That's because being rich is a state of mind and having a set of behaviors. If the economy were to start over, those people who followed the habits that tend to make people rich would be the ones becoming rich again in the new economy.

Short-term thinking is a poverty mindset

Meanwhile, people with a poverty mindset would remain poor the second time around. One of the characteristics of a poverty mindset was illustrated in the marshmallow test. The poverty mindset is one where people are not able to delay gratification for a future reward. People with this kind of mindset are not going to go to college and get a degree in a useful field so they can have a job four or five years from now, even if college is free. You have to address the mindset first.

You can also give people with a poverty mindset a huge amount of money, and they are going to blow it off because of their short-term thinking patterns. If you think long-term, you're going to recognize that a few million dollars can be blown off like that and you're better off investing most of it. But if you have a poverty mindset, you won't be thinking about what happens to the money five years from now. You'll be spending the money as fast as you can spend it. This happens all the time in real life. Good examples are lottery winners, most of who end up broke a few years after cashing in. Many athletes who become rich end up broke for the same reason. They haven't yet learned to think in terms that involve delayed gratification and long-term thinking, so can't handle the money that they are making.

The tension of survival

One thing about life is that you need to take care of your immediate needs first. That means procuring food and shelter. The requirement that we have to satisfy our immediate needs first has roots way back into the animal kingdom. So, this is a pretty hardwired trait. It's only in recent evolution that human beings have developed a sense of long-term outcomes.

Given the recent arrival on the scene of this kind of thinking, it's not surprising that many people have difficulty with it. It's something that you have to learn in many cases.

So, there is always a tension that exists between satisfying your needs in the now and your long-term interests. This tension can be enhanced by some very real-world concerns, such as having to pay your rent and get enough food to eat.

However, often, that misses the forest for the trees. People fail to think of ways they can trade a little bit of pain now for more pleasure or security in the future. This tension plays out well beyond meeting your own personal needs. Many new businesses fail because budding entrepreneurs are only thinking short-term. So, maybe they save money that could have been spent on expensive promotional campaigns, but they might also be missing out on big-ticket sales that could take their business to the next level.

How to become a long-term thinker

One of the challenges of becoming successful is to truly become a long-term thinker. Like any habit at first, becoming a long-term thinker is going to require conscious effort, and conscious effort takes energy.

If you suffer from the "short-term thinking" disease, you can develop your long-term thinking in steps by gradually increasing your time horizon. As always, one of the best strategies is to break down your goals into smaller sub-goals that can be achieved in various amounts of time. That way, something that takes a year to accomplish could be broken down into some tasks that need to be done now, some in a few weeks and some in a month.

Visualization can be a key exercise when learning to be a long-term thinker. Try seeing yourself in the future benefiting from the sacrifices you are making now in exchange for a better tomorrow. Visualization helps train the subconscious for dealing with the denial that must happen in the near-term in order to obtain results down the road.

Another characteristic of a long-term thinker is they recognize that a price has to be paid for everything. You can avoid short-term pain now, but that price will still have to be paid later – that is, the price you have to pay increases with time if you don't start paying it now. An example we can use is missing a car payment. Suppose you have a new car with a $300 a month payment. One month, you're tight on cash and really want to join your friends in Las Vegas for a fun vacation. You decide to take the trip and spend the money you were going to use for the car payment. You say, no worries, you'll catch up later. Then, for some reason, you miss the second payment. By the third month, you're facing repossession, and now, you have to come up with $900 instead of $300 for the car. Had you been a long-term thinker, at the very least, you would have passed on the Vegas trip and said, "next time." Or maybe, you would have worked some extra hours so that you could have been in a position to pay for the trip and the car.

That is the price of self-denial that often must be paid in order to reap benefits later. You might have to pay the price of self-denial in many ways. Maybe, when your friends are out enjoying the weekend on a Friday night, if you have a new business, you're putting some extra hours in so that you can make more money the following month. Or maybe, you're looking to buy a house, so you stopped eating out so that you could save extra money toward a downpayment over the course of a year.

Are you a long-term thinker? Many people think they are, but they really aren't. Start looking at the goals you have in your life that you can't meet. Are you always trying to lose weight and never succeeding?

Have you pledged to save money for an emergency fund but it's still sitting at $0? Did you commit to going back to school, but somehow, never got around to it? If you can write down a list of goals like this that you aren't meeting, then maybe you haven't mastered the art of long-term thinking and the price of self-denial.

People always have plans, but they are often vague

Everyone has dreams. I am sure that it's a rare person who couldn't tell you about some dream they have for the future. So, what is different about all these people who are never realizing those dreams as compared to the successful who are always nailing down every goal they set?

One characteristic that stands out is how well you have planned for your long-term goals. There is a big difference between a goal and a dream. A goal is something that you plan out, schedule, and act on. A dream is a wistful hope – something that will "happen" to you "someday." Successful people don't have hopes and dreams, they have specific goals, and they develop and carry out plans to meet them. And those plans are built-up in detail.

As always, use the tool of writing things down. Start by writing your long-term goal that will take a long time to realize, broken down into the constituent sub-goals. Then, put together a schedule so that you can achieve each of the sub-goals by specific dates. In order to actually turn your goal into an achievement that has been realized, you will need to have sub-goals that are realistic, and you will also have to have a constant schedule where you are meeting your goals on a regular basis.

Also, look at things from an angle of what price you will have to pay in each instance. There is going to be a price for the overall goal, but there are also going to be prices that need to be paid for the sub-goals.

Maybe they are the same price broken down into small chunks, but you need to have it spelled out what the price is going to be. Are you going to have to work an extra two hours a day? Save money? Spend time away from home? People who are not successful and spend their lives with hopes and dreams don't know the price they would have to pay in order to realize their goals.

Train yourself to start thinking long-term not only by setting goals, but making specific plans and getting the price that has to be paid in specific terms. Then act on your plans.

Chapter 8: Habits of the Unsuccessful

It's great to spend time thinking about the habits of the rich and successful, but what about the habits of the unsuccessful? We've already touched on a few, but it can be enlightening, actually, to focus on traits that keep people from being successful. One way to become more successful in your life is to simply look at what the unsuccessful are doing and do the opposite or adopt opposite habits.

Making Excuses

Making excuses for everything is a classic character trait that unsuccessful people have. The unsuccessful person is stuck in a rut, and there are a million reasons why. They can be grand – it's the fault of the 1%, it's the stupid economy, or it's the President. Or they can be closer to home, but the key theme that runs through the mentality of someone who is unsuccessful is that they are a victim and not really in control of their lives. Everyone is responsible for their position in life except the person who is the one doing the complaining. Someone who has this mentality is not someone who is taking responsibility for their lives. Taking responsibility means owning your outcomes, not just making decisions. Excuses allow people to shirk responsibility because, then, it's someone else's fault or pure luck that put our unfortunate victim in the position where they are. The fact is that we are all where we are because of the choices that we have made. And choices have an impact that is similar to compound interest. If you make one bad decision and then another, they start adding up until you find yourself trapped in a real bind.

One thing people often say to defend themselves is that life isn't fair. And honestly, sometimes, it's not, but it's not fair for any of us. You can sit there feeling sorry for yourself and say it's your lack of education, it's the President destroying jobs, or whatever, but that isn't going to change anything. Only you can change the situation that you find yourself in, and you do that by taking action.

This can be a painful process emotionally. For someone who has been blaming others for their fate, taking responsibility means admitting to themselves that they have made decisions that put them where they are today, and it wasn't because of the actions of other people. That might be too hard for some people to admit to themselves, and as a result, they may never change. But if you can take that first step, you can be on the road to success. Successful people in the world know that they are in control, and they accept responsibility when things don't work out.

Are you making excuses? If you are making excuses, one way to retrain yourself is to do the opposite of the excuse. Of course, taking action in this manner will require some discipline. Let's look at some common excuses people make for their situation.

I'm not smart enough

This is one of the most common excuses ever thrown about. Yes, it's true that some people are "smarter" than others – that may mean that they can learn faster or do less work to get by. But there are ways to make up for not being in the top echelon by working harder and putting extra effort. Everyone brings their own talents as well. For example, you might hear that someone is not "smart enough" to become a doctor. Smarts may be important when it comes to passing the MCAT or acing med school classes without much effort, but being an actual doctor rather than a med student actually relies on many different skills. Many of those are people skills and the ability to listen. Or a surgeon has to be able to work with their hands, not just be "book smart." Instead of dismissing something as an impossibility, take a look at what you bring to the table and ask yourself how you can compensate for your weaknesses. But often, our weaknesses are more a perception than reality. If you're not as fast as someone else at memorization, what difference does it make? None. You can make up for it by working harder, and when you've graduated, it won't matter at all.

I'm too old

This is possibly the most common excuse people use not to make changes in their lives. And it can be used surprisingly early. The fact is that being too old isn't an excuse unless you're talking about trying out for something that has a real age limit. Becoming a professional football player or joining the military have real age limits, but becoming successful knows no limits at all. If you want to become an entrepreneur, or change your career, or become a professional by going to law school or medical school, there is no time like the present. Sure, it's true you could come up with all kinds of excuses as to why you can't do it, but why not live life to your fullest potential instead? Many entrepreneurs and change agents are in their fifties and beyond. Don't use age as an excuse unless there is a genuine reason for it.

I'll start tomorrow

This is the kind of excuse someone prone to procrastination may make. If they are overweight, they'll start the diet tomorrow. If they aren't making enough money to pay the bills, they'll look for a new job next month. If someone has an exciting business idea that they are interested in, well, they will get that started "someday." Putting off things with the excuse that you'll take care of it "tomorrow" is one of the oldest bad habits in the book, and it's one you need to get rid of as soon as possible. If this is a habit, it's going to take effort to relearn how to behave and replace it with better habits, so you will have to put a lot of conscious effort now into changing your behavior. You can get started right away. Do you have a phone call that you have to make that you're putting off because it makes you uncomfortable? Make that call today instead of tomorrow. Is there an appointment that you're trying to push off into the future? Change direction and get that appointment scheduled as quickly as possible (and don't cancel).

I don't have enough education

The internet is full of resources and opportunities to learn. You can start with free resources like the Kahn Academy on YouTube, and take low-cost courses on Udemy. Many universities offer online degrees across a wide variety of fields. If you are interested in becoming an entrepreneur, a degree doesn't even matter. What matters is what you actually know, so you can leverage the free and low-cost resources on the internet in order to get the knowledge that you need to succeed. In any case, if you lack the education you need to fulfill some dream you've had, stop making excuses, and get that education.

I'm too busy

We get it. You're busy with your family life and your job. You can use that as an excuse if it suits you, and you'll be exactly where you're at now in five years. Or, you can get up an hour earlier in the morning and use that extra time to make headway in transforming the direction of your life. If you are busy, make a schedule and schedule time to work on new projects.

It takes money to make money

One of the oldest myths in the book and one of the most convenient for people who have unhealthy habits that are looking for an excuse. These days, this old myth is less true than it's ever been. The fact is that you can create a business for next to nothing by leveraging the internet, smartphone apps, blogs, and other tools. Globalization of labor means that if you need to, you can hire talent globally at low cost.

The bottom line

The bottom line when it comes to excuses is an old adage – that thoughts are things. That is, you create your own reality via thoughts. The 50-year-old that says they are too old to attend law school is never going to attend law school. By giving in to the too-old myth and the thoughts surrounding that excuse, they have created a reality where they are not going to be attending law school. Meanwhile, the 50-year old who says "law school is hard, and because of my age and family commitments, it's going to be a little bit harder, but I am going anyway" is the one who is going to be a lawyer 4 years later.

Gossiping and complaining

Another habit of being unsuccessful is constant complaining. If you meet someone at a party and they are complaining about this and that and why it's holding them back, this is not someone you want to emulate. People who aren't successful often gossip about others as well, because when you're not successful, you can be filled with envy and resentment, as well as jealousy. When those emotions govern how you feel about other people's success, then you can deal with it by talking about them to make them look bad.

Complaining also reflects underlying attitudes. For example, one of the attitudes that complaining can reflect is hopelessness. We've used this example before, but let's return to the situation of owing back taxes. John owes $40,000 in back taxes he accumulated while working as a contractor, but he suddenly had his contract canceled and couldn't raise the money to pay it off. However, John worked hard to find new jobs, and then once his income got going again, he sat down with a tax advisor to work out a payment plan to present to the IRS. Meanwhile, his cousin Jack also racked up a $40,000 tax debt, but when you meet Jack at a party, all he does is complain about the IRS, often saying that taxes are illegal and he shouldn't have to pay them. He has a thousand stories about how the IRS abuses people, but he doesn't have one minute of planning to deal with his tax debt. John made some mistakes but is adopting the habits of the successful and moving on. Jack is wallowing in his failures and plans to stay there.

Of course, everyone complains, and part of the process of changing your habits so that you can be more successful is to take a step back and think about what you are complaining about. Complaining is a bad habit because it turns you into a victim, and therefore, relieves you of responsibility for changing the situation that is generating the complaining. This kind of behavior also creates negative energy that will prevent you from pursuing a more successful path in life. Negative energy can be draining, and it will feed other situations in a way that you start making excuses in other areas of life. Complaining also takes up time – time that could be spent on directing your mind towards more productive purposes.

The Quitter

Remember, I told you about the problems I was having in college, as a result of my chronic lateness problem? After flunking out, I could have quit. I saw a fair number of people quit either college or a tough major. I had a friend that jumped through multiple hoops to get into law school, including writing a letter to the dean begging to be admitted and listing multiple reasons why he should be admitted despite his slightly lower than average GPA. The letter convinced the dean, and they admitted him. He went to class for a month and then quit.

Being a quitter isn't the quality of a successful person. Finishing what you start is the opposite quality, and successful people finish what they start. That isn't to say that you should be forced to stay the course in every single endeavor, driving it straight into the ground even if it's a failing business or something you're just not suited for. What we are looking for in these bad habits isn't a once-or-twice kind of thing but rather a pattern. Someone who isn't successful is exhibiting bad habits over and over again. So, they aren't just late to one or two meetings; they are chronically late. They don't just quit the baseball team; they quit virtually everything they get involved with. But generally speaking, one thing that we know is true is that quitters are not winners.

Being Late

I started this book off explaining the consequences I endured for being late. And it was no accident that I selected that as an example. Being late is a trait of the unsuccessful. When you are late all the time, you are exhibiting multiple problems. The first one is an inability to manage your time. To reach the top and be successful, you have to be efficient at managing your own time. You will also have to respect the deadlines of others. If you are late all the time, it illustrates that you don't care about the schedules of others. For example, if someone has agreed to meet you to discuss a business deal at 1 PM, but you show up at 1:20 PM, you've wasted 20 minutes of their time. That is the time that they've carved out of their busy schedule for YOU. But you disrespected their time, so please forgive them if they feel like you are disrespecting them personally. If it happens repeatedly, it shows you can't be relied on. It also might reflect that you are someone who puts something off to the last minute, which is the classic procrastinator. If you are late to meetings, you're probably late starting projects. People who are repeatedly late often overestimate their ability to get projects done quickly and so, wait far too long to get started on them. Do you want someone like that on your team? Someone who is late for you means that clients won't be getting the expected goods on the dates they want them delivered.

If you are someone who is repeatedly late for everything, fixing this one very bad habit can go a long way toward changing the direction of your life generally. If you are late because you are inconsiderate of others' time, perhaps showing contempt, you might take a time out and figure out why you have that attitude. It also shows that others you are meeting with are not important to you (at least, it looks that way to them). People who are chronically late also tend to have other problems like being late paying their bills. That is an attitude and behavior that needs correcting. If you are late because you are a sloppy time manager, that will be an easier fix. Start by making sure you show up early by five minutes to meetings, even if it's just a social occasion. Instead of making your friends wait for you at lunch all the time, make sure you're always there right on time. You will be surprised at how much they appreciate you and the increased respect that this will garner. You will also find that when you start showing up on time or early to meetings, this will reverberate through your work and home life. You will stop procrastinating and start your projects early rather than at the last minute, whether it's a software program you're designing for your business or raking the leaves in the backyard.

In short, being someone who is chronically late means that you are someone who has a seriously bad habit. Fixing this bad habit is something to make a priority on.

Living in the moment

A lot of gurus these days say we should "live in the now." Maybe that is true to some extent, and we will address that in the next bad habit, but if you are living in the moment without any regard to the future, then you have a bad habit that is in need of fixing. One of the consequences of living in the moment is bad money handling. People who are living in the moment spend what they have without any regard to how much money they are going to need in the future, and they develop financial problems as a result. This can be bad or very bad depending on circumstances. Going on a spending splurge at the mall and leave yourself with only $50 left for the rest of the week might be bad, but getting a payday loan that has a high interest payment for the next 12 months, or buying a new car when it's outside your budget but they approve the loan anyway – these are both decisions that show you are living in the now far too much without regard to future financial pain. People who are trapped in living in the moment are unable to delay gratification. If this describes your situation, then you need to step back and learn how to spend within your limits, and start bypassing things that you "want." You also need to spend some time planning for the future.

Wasting Time

We've already touched upon this one, but unsuccessful people are masters at wasting time. While a successful person is going to put in the extra time and effort to get what they need to get done finished, the unsuccessful person will prefer to watch television and play video games instead. When the successful person gets up early in the morning to put an extra hour into a new business venture, the unsuccessful person not only stays in bed, they sleep an hour later than they need to. If faced with a choice between working an extra hour in the evening or going out with buddies to slam beers, the unsuccessful person always opts for the beer.

Procrastination

The person who puts things off is a classically
unsuccessful person. You probably met some of them
in school, or maybe when you were in school, you
were one of those people yourself. The fact is that
tasks that you need to get done in life take a certain
amount of time, no matter how smart or gifted you
are. A procrastinator will put off studying for a test
until the last minute. Sometimes, they might pull that
off. But do you think you will be a successful
businessman or woman pulling those kinds of stunts
in the real world?

Putting things off can have a real cost. It can mean
that you don't get important projects done on time. It
can mean that you are cutting into the time of others
when they depend on you. If you procrastinate on
implementing your dreams and plans, it can mean that
your new business idea never gets started.

Sometimes, procrastinators overestimate their own abilities. So, they actually believe that they can get a massive project done in a short time period. Other times, they are simply lazy. Procrastination can cut across the board for many people that have this character flaw, with the procrastinator falling behind on bills, work projects, doctor's appointments, and paying taxes, among other things. In short, people who procrastinate are people who live by the old Mexican phrase, "hasta manana", that is, "see you tomorrow". The problem is that you can run out of "tomorrows", so you need to get in the habit of doing it now, not tomorrow.

The bad habit of procrastination is really another version of being trapped in short-term versus long-term thinking, but if you suffer from this bad habit, you need to examine what problems and issues might be underlying it.

When it comes to procrastination regarding new business ideas and things of that nature, people who procrastinate are unlikely to ever launch their business. Remember that phrase – "there is no time like the present".

All Talk, No Action

In the Bible, it says, "You will know them by their fruits." When it comes to success, this is definitely true. If you meet someone and they can talk up a storm all day about this and that, but they have never done this or that, or they tried and failed, then you know this is someone who is unsuccessful. The fact is if you talk a lot but get nothing done, then you're unsuccessful. A cool person is a person of action. When they talk about something, they make it happen. If you are talking about a lot of things, ideas, business ventures, and so forth, but they never seem to materialize, take a step back and find out why. Are you a procrastinator (see above)? There is some

underlying reason why you're all talk and no action.
Fix the underlying reason first.

Chapter 9: Digital Decluttering

These days, we are surrounded by distractions to a level that has never been seen before. An endless array of entertainment options exists, from Netflix to regular TV, to video games to movies. People – adults – are now spending time during their day playing video games on their smartphones. Even before the advent of the digital world, people were already spending large amounts of time watching television.

Of course, we aren't saying you should completely abandon all your friends on Facebook or never enjoy yourself playing a video game, but the old adage remains true today – "All things in moderation". You also have to ask yourself how much time the successful devote to such pursuits. Do you think that Jeff Bezos and Tim Cook are sitting around playing video games and checking Facebook? They probably have better things to do – and so do you.

Schedule your downtime

One of the ways you can remain connected and also stay productive is to schedule downtime to relax. This can include all things involving relaxation – not just digital, but you can schedule breaks in between your work, for example, to look at Facebook or whatever digital activity you are obsessed with. But quite frankly, you are going to be better off the less time you spend on such pursuits. Harsh but true.

Do you really benefit from watching so much Netflix?

Maybe your friends are binge-watching Netflix or other digital TV outlets. That doesn't mean that you should, too. If you want to be successful, you need to devote more time to learning and preparation and less time to mindless recreation. That means you should be spending time reading more books about successful habits, success in business, and learning all you can about your particular industry. We live in the knowledge age, and those who know the most about their area of expertise are going to be the ones that are rewarded. You can make a choice: Do you want to excel in your career or business, or would you rather catch an extra hour of Netflix?

Cut back on accounts

I have to admit that I began developing a Twitter addiction a few years ago, and found myself constantly checking Twitter and getting into arguments with people on Twitter when I could have used that time far more productively. At the time, of course, I was using other social media outlets, which of course included Facebook, as well as reading many news websites and wasting time on their comment boards.

I realized that it didn't matter what people I didn't even know thought about on Twitter and that the illusion of a "town square" is just that. So, I decided to cut out Twitter altogether. I also decided to cancel multiple subscriptions to news websites so that I wouldn't be tempted to waste time commenting on the articles. I also initially decided to cut down my Facebook time in half, but a few months later, I found I was only rarely logging onto the site. I still have an account, but these days, I only use it for business purposes or on the occasion that someone sends me a private message through Facebook.

When you begin cutting back on these accounts, you are going to find that social media is not as important as you thought it was. Most of it is nothing more than a distraction, and successful people don't let distractions rule their lives. You have to make your own personal decisions. You can choose which sites are the most important to you and settle on time limits that you can live with. Using some sites for business purposes is necessary – for example, many people need to carry on with Facebook Advertising to promote their business interests. However, be careful with your evaluations. It's far too easy to lie to yourself about needing an account for a site that you're addicted to, but in actuality, serves no real useful purpose.

Unsubscribe from unnecessary Email Newsletters

While all the focus is on Facebook and Twitter, the old school methods of using digital to take up our time are alive and well. One of these methods is the digital newsletter. You cannot visit a website without facing demands that you give them your email address so they can send you tips in your email inbox. Now, again, I am not saying you should never sign up for a newsletter. It may be useful, and people may be offering products for sale which you have a genuine interest in. But how many newsletters are you signed up for that you really don't need? The simple fact that your inbox may be crowded with large numbers of "newsletters" is a bad habit – because all that crowding can cause you to miss important emails. Do a regular evaluation of email newsletters and unsubscribe from the ones you really don't need. Remember that every second in your life counts and time spent wasted reading newsletters that aren't all that important is time that could be better spent on productive purposes.

Organize your computer

One of the problems I used to have was that my computer was completely disorganized. Given the important role that computers play in the modern business world, this can be a major productivity issue. The time you are wasting trying to find a file that you have no idea where you put it is the time that your competition is spending beating you.

Start by organizing your files on the desktop and in your Downloads Folder. I have a new theory that you can spot unsuccessful people by looking at how their computer is organized. If someone has a desktop and downloads folders that are filled with huge numbers of files, that can be a mark of an unsuccessful person because it shows a lack of organizational skills. It should go without saying that you should have your folders on your main drive well-organized. When you download something, there is no reason for it to remain in your Downloads Folder. You should either move it to the appropriate folder on your main drive or if it's not going to be useful, delete it. The same goes for your desktop – a place where some people feel they can store gobs of files. Then later, when you ask them for a particular file, they have huge problems trying to track it down. That is nothing more than a waste of time.

Keep your computer operating in optimal condition

Make sure that you are not only keeping your hard disk organized as far as folders and where files are stored; make sure that you regularly defrag your disk. There are many disk cleaning programs that are available in places like the Mac app store that can help you keep your disk organized in top shape. An inefficient computer is going to make you inefficient with the extra time required to get things accomplished.

Delete bookmarks you no longer use

It's all too easy to bookmark a website that we think is super important, only to find out later that we're never using it. If your browser has a large number of bookmarks, you should spend some time going through and getting rid of those you are no longer using. It may seem like a small thing, but the reality of life is that there is not a second to waste. Your life is temporary and you have even less time to work productively and generate success and the money that goes along with it. Cutting out unused bookmarks is a small way to increase your productivity because it will make finding the bookmarks that you actually need that much easier.

Limit Smartphone Availability

I will put this in the "last but not least" category. In fact, it's dreadfully important.

In the past decade, we've literally become addicted to our smartphones. Text messaging have become the de facto communication method. While it's convenient and immediate, the problem is that it's a distraction. You are going to have a hard time doing this, but when you're working on important projects, you need to lose the smartphone. Incoming text messages (and messages from Facebook, if you have that on there, too) are a major cause of workflow interruptions. This is another issue that comes up with short-term vs. long-term thinking, and whether you need instant gratification or are able to put things off to the future. The reality is if you think that your Facebook friends and endless text messages are more important than your work, then you are not going to be nearly as successful as you are going to be. You have to accept the reality of the world – that you are going to need to be unavailable for stretches of time. Productive people - the most successful people - are not going to be letting themselves get distracted by every little thought or whim when people feel they need to communicate with them. You can put that stuff off for a while when you are in the midst of important work. Consider shutting your phone off, or if you work in an office, leave the phone in your car for long periods of time. There are very few things that can't wait 60 minutes to an hour or two in order to check, and the reality is that most of our communications are frivolous. So, let them wait. Work now, and socialize later.

Turn off notifications

If you are like me, you have tons of apps on your devices. With the rise of free apps in the app stores, it makes it all too easy to download something just to try it out. In fact, my devices were once full of apps that I didn't use at all – that is until I decided to declutter my smartphone and iPad. Delete apps that you aren't using and organize the ones that you are so that things you need are easy to find. You should also turn off notifications – especially from games. Notifications from apps can be another major distraction, especially if the notification is from the app itself. Its one thing to get a text message from a child or your spouse, and quite another to be interrupted by a message from a game on your phone.

Minimize email accounts

Are you one of these people that now have multiple email accounts? You should only really require two. You should have a business email account and a personal email account. If you have ten email accounts, you really need to ask yourself what purpose they are serving. Now, there are some cases where a genuine purpose is served. For example, I have multiple businesses, and some of them have their own email accounts. But rather than reading a large number of different email accounts, try and see if you can set up forwarding, so that you have one master business email account that you check on a regular basis and emails that are inbound to the other accounts get forwarded to your main one so that you can read everything in a central location. The more organized and streamlined you are, the more productive you are going to be.

Chapter 10: Changing Your Social Circle

This one is sure to fan the flames. But have you considered that you take on the habits of the people you associate with? A friend of mine in college actually put this in blunt terms. He said – and pardon my language: "If you hang around assholes, you become an asshole". He stated it crudely, but it's a fundamental truth. The people that you spend most of your time with are going to be the people who rub off on you and the people whom you emulate. A lot of this even happens on a subconscious level.

We are more cognizant of the issues surrounding choosing our friends in our youth. If you want to become a doctor when you are 20-years-old, do you think hanging around old friends from high school who are heroin addicts is going to be a productive path? You will be constantly tempted to use drugs by your friends, who will also be mocking your study habits. Some of us are strong enough to weather this, but most of us are going to be influenced by it, and find ourselves studying a bit less, or maybe even a lot less.

If you want to lose weight and exercise, would it be productive to hang out with a group of overweight people that eat a junk food diet and don't like exercise? Or would you be better off hanging around motivated, fit people that work out hard at the gym, and eat healthy diets? Obviously, the latter is more congruent with your goals, and more likely to help you strive for your own success.

The fact is that people's motivations and habits are contagious. As was said earlier, we're more aware of this when we are younger and your parents probably warned you about "running around in the wrong circle" in recognition of this undeniable fact of life. However, we are also susceptible to this as adults. It's true that our personalities are more hardened as adults, but you wouldn't be reading this if you didn't need to change your direction, and so this is an important issue for you.

People that you associate with are impacting you in dramatic and subtle ways: They can change your belief systems, what you value the most, attitudes toward money and education, and how you spend your money. They can impact nearly every aspect of your mind and personality. If you are trying to lead a life of self-discipline and delayed gratification, hanging around a bunch of freeloaders is not going to help you live the kind of life you're hoping for. In fact, they may be feeding off your energy and might bring your life down in the process.

The subconscious is able to pick up on the habits of others. And it's perfectly capable of picking up bad habits. If you hang around people that are either not going anywhere or worse, leading destructive lifestyles, your subconscious is liable to pick this up and incorporate their habits into your own life.

If you want contagious behaviors, energy, and beliefs that will help you, find successful people to spend your time with. You'll not only find that you can emulate them and absorb their emotions and energy, but they may also be interested in directly helping you reach your goals. You could even find people to bounce ideas off of that might offer to help finance your new business, or they may have connections to help you get jobs or get into school, or whatever you are interested in pursuing.

If you are finding that your current circle of friends isn't cutting it, then you need to branch out and look for people who are already successful. You're going to find that they are more interesting and exciting, to begin with. They are also going to be more optimistic. Unsuccessful people don't tend to be optimistic. Over the long-term, they don't tend to be interesting either.

I say this as a result of my own experiences. You will be surprised at the number of super smart people who are unsuccessful. When you first meet them, they can weave many tales that are interesting, and they sound well-read (and maybe they are). But at their core, they have many serious attitude problems, some of which may stem from their inherent abilities. Being intelligent, many disdain having to work for something, and they may refuse to apply themselves. They may not like work and feel they are intellectually superior, and so express contempt for the "system." Trust me, these are not the kinds of people that you want to be associating with, either. They are as destructive as your nearest heroin addicts.

So whatever you do next, start making friends with more successful people. Find people who have goals that are more like yours.

Chapter 11: Inspiring Quotes

In this chapter, we've included some inspiring quotes related to the many issues we have discussed. They can also serve as affirmations.

William Shakespeare

Better three hours too soon, than one minute too late.

Maya Angelou

Courage is the most important of all the virtues because, without courage, you can't practice any other virtue consistently.

Benjamin Franklin

Many people die at twenty-five and aren't buried until they are seventy-five.

Well done is better than well said.

Being ignorant is not so much a shame, as being unwilling to learn.

Lost Time is never found again.

You may delay, but time will not.

He that rises late must trot all day.

Steve Jobs

Remembering that I'll be dead soon is the most important tool I've ever encountered to help me make the big choices in life.

Your work is going to fill a large part of your life, and the only way to be truly satisfied is to do what you believe is great work. And the only way to do great work is to love what you do. If you haven't found it yet, keep looking. Don't settle. As with all matters of the heart, you'll know when you find it.

Remembering that you are going to die is the best way I know to avoid the trap of thinking you have something to lose. You are already naked. There is no reason not to follow your heart.

Oprah Winfrey

Surround yourself with only people who are going to lift you higher.

The biggest adventure you can ever take is to live the life of your dreams.

Doing the best at this moment puts you in the best place for the next moment.

Tony Robbins

Setting goals is the first step in turning the invisible into the visible.

The path to success is to take massive, determined action.

The quality of your life is the quality of your relationships.

Chapter 12: Other Tips

In this chapter, we'll share some more tips about adopting the habits of successful people.

Avoid Vices

We spent some time discussing time wasted in front of the television screen or playing video games. Another time waster (and possible money waster) that separates the successful from the unsuccessful is time devoted to traditional vices. We can start with drug use. Now, it's possible that some people are going to be drug users and still be successful, but people like that are the exception rather than the rule. The vast majority of drug users are failures, period; and the vast majority of successful people are not drug users.

When you become a drug user, no matter how modest the drug, it takes on a life of its own. People who become addicted to drugs find that, soon enough, their life is revolving around the drug. Do you think that you're going to be successful if the focus in life is marijuana, cocaine, or opiates? My bet is you'll find that success is elusive if you're devoting time to getting "high."

The same goes for drinking. If you're an alcoholic, one of the primary focuses in your life, if not the primary focus, depending on how severe your problem is, will be alcohol itself. Your drinking is not only going to consume a great deal of your life, but it's also going to shape the people that you associate with. One thing I discovered in adulthood is that many low-level alcoholics spend a large amount of their time in local bars. Typically, they'll be at one bar or another "having a few beers" nearly every single night of the week. Let me clue you in on this if you haven't figured this out already: The successful amongst us aren't spending their time at night getting wasted at neighborhood bars.

That isn't to say that perhaps smoking marijuana once in a while or drinking alcohol in moderation can't be done as part of a successful life. It can, but it's important to be aware of the potential pitfalls that can result if your usage becomes a problem. This can be true, especially in the case of marijuana, when many users are in denial about its destructive impacts.

Another important vice is gambling, and unfortunately, our wise politicians have made gambling more accessible as the years go by. Many Native American tribes cleverly latched onto gambling casinos as a way to generate revenue. That was smart on their part, and if you can gamble now and then for entertainment purposes, that is fine, along the same lines that moderate drinking or occasional marijuana isn't going to blow up your life. However, be aware that many people find gambling addictive, and it can become a huge problem – it can literally destroy your entire life. There used to be a show called "*Intervention*," and one episode that stood out for me was a childhood prodigy who was teaching medical school classes as a teenager. When he got older, he started visiting gambling casinos and became addicted. It literally completely destroyed his life. It turned him into an obnoxious jerk, and he was constantly desperate because he owed many shady people large sums of money, and he was so addicted to gambling that that was all he thought about. So, here was someone who could have been extremely successful as a professor or as a doctor, and yet he threw it all way for a gambling addiction. I often wonder where he is at now, but I am afraid to look. Overcoming an addiction like that is extremely difficult. I'd say it's best not to start gambling in the first place.

Meditation

One thing that the most successful people spend time on daily is meditation. It can help clear the mind and bring in focus. Many successful people incorporate a few minutes of daily meditation into their morning routine. If you are religious, you can use morning prayers for the same purpose.

Exercise

Staying physically fit is very important for the successful. Of course, not all of them do it, but let me tell you: It's something that will improve your life. You will find that you have more focus and energy if you exercise on a regular basis. It's better to have more vigorous exercise than not, but simply walking every day is a huge improvement over being sedentary. You should also include some strength training at least a couple of days per week. Many of the most successful people also incorporate exercise into their morning routine. It's a great way to wake up the body without depending on caffeine or other artificial measures. People that exercise in the early morning hours include Richard Branson, Mick Jagger, Michelle Obama, and Howard Schultz. One way to organize your early morning hours could be meditation to begin with, and follow that with an hour of vigorous exercise.

Stop Complaining, Blaming, and Maiming

We've talked about some of these issues before – the complaining, blaming, and maiming people are those who are unsuccessful. But let's face facts: If you are having problems in your professional and business life or have financial issues, there is only one person to look to, and that's you. The fact is you got to where you are by the choices that you have made in your life up to this point. Acknowledging this might be painful, but that's the first step toward recovery. When you admit that it's not the economy, not some corporation, not the "1%" that is keeping you down but it's your own actions that are keeping you down, then it's going to be easier to begin reversing course and taking control of your own life.

The fact is, you are in the driver's seat. So, stop pretending that other people, whether it's the government or your boss or whoever, are in control of your life's direction. You are the one who controls where this life heads. You can choose to pretend that others are in control. That is a nice fantasy that will, in the end, leave you staying in a place where you are now (or declining), but it's not reality. People that don't share the victim mentality are charting their own course forward.

As we've discussed before, complaining is not a productive activity. For one, it's a waste of energy. It solves nothing, and the negative energy creates a feedback loop. If you complain about being broke or negative relationships at work, you're actually amplifying the negative energy, which ensures that you're going to get more of what you claim you're trying to avoid – you're going to find more financial problems and more difficulties in your relationships at the office.

The more negative you are, the more you're going to bring those around you down to your level. Your negative attitudes are going hurt others in the process, whether by your failure to live up to the life you could have lived, or by becoming needy and destructive.

Start replacing your complaints with positive affirmations, even if they are difficult to believe at first. The energy you put out to the universe is the energy you are going to receive back. So, if you spend your time saying "the 1% are stealing all the money, so they're keeping me down", replace that with "I live in a universe of abundance and wealth is entering into my life". You can think up your own positive affirmations about money or whatever issues are challenging you. Search online if you have trouble coming up with them.

Perhaps, the core concept that you need to adopt if complaining, blaming, and maiming describes your situation, is that reality is created by one's thoughts.

Don't think it's true? What is the iPhone, if nothing more than a thought? At one time, maybe 12-15 years ago, the entire concept was nothing more than a thought that existed in the mind of Steve Jobs. The very chair you are sitting on was at one time, just a thought. Minds control the universe, and thoughts create reality. You can use your thoughts to swim around in your misery and self-pity, or you can think optimistic, positive thoughts that will help you overcome life's difficulties and find success.

Committing to change with a timeline

As we've discussed before, you can create long-term and short-term goals. Often, they can really be both the same goal or directed at satisfying the same goal. You should make scheduled plans to carry out your goals and break them down into sub-goals that are easy to meet within realistic time frames. Of course, this isn't something that is going to be set in stone. Unforeseen obstacles may arise that require you to adjust your timeline and goals.

Think, write, read, and rewrite

Remember that through our thoughts, we create our external reality. You begin your own personal reality with your own thoughts. So why not choose to think positive thoughts? Think about what you want to create in your own life, and then begin by writing your thoughts down on paper. Once you've written a thought down on paper, that thought has become manifested in the physical world, and has become "real" in the conventional sense. Read and rewrite your thoughts to refine them into realizable goals that can be carried forward into a practical plan. Then TAKE ACTION. When it comes to any endeavor, anyone can show you what to do. Go on YouTube, and there are thousands of videos made by successful people that teach others how to make money. But sadly, 99% of the people that watch these instructional videos will never take action. The same is true with self-help books. A lot of people will read the books, but few will ever act on them, even though now they have the information they need in order to change their lives. When it comes down to it, change is always up to you. Nobody else can change your life for you. If you want to join the "1%", I would suggest you start by joining the 1% who actually take action and get things done in their lives. Don't be among the rest of people that remain languishing in the world of the unsuccessful.

Conclusion

Thank you for taking the time to read *11 Secret Habits of Successful People*.

I hope that you have found this book useful and that some of my suggestions on how to improve success in your life are practical for you to implement. I challenge you right now to do far more than simply read this book and then put it away. My challenge to you is that you take action and put the lessons of this book into practice.

Remember our discussion about procrastination – there is no time to delay. You must put it in action NOW, or your life will never change.

Too many people simply drift through life, never living up to their full potential. Are you one of them? Or are you going to start adopting the life lessons and habits of the successful and change the direction of your life?

What happens now is entirely up to you. Nobody can force you to make changes in your life, but you should be aware that you are in the driver's seat and nobody else is controlling your fate – not your boss, not the President, not a large corporation and least of all, the rich. You, and only you, will determine how much success you have.

I sincerely wish you good luck on your journey. I hope you enjoyed the book, and would like to thank you ahead of time for reviewing it! Good luck!

Connect with us on our Facebook page
www.facebook.com/bluesourceandfriends and stay
tuned to our latest book promotions and free
giveaways.